FREEMANS

FREEMANS

Food and Drink | Interiors | Grooming | Style

TAAVO SOMER WITH DAVID COGGINS

HARPER DESIGN
An Imprint of HarperCollins Publishers

CONTENTS

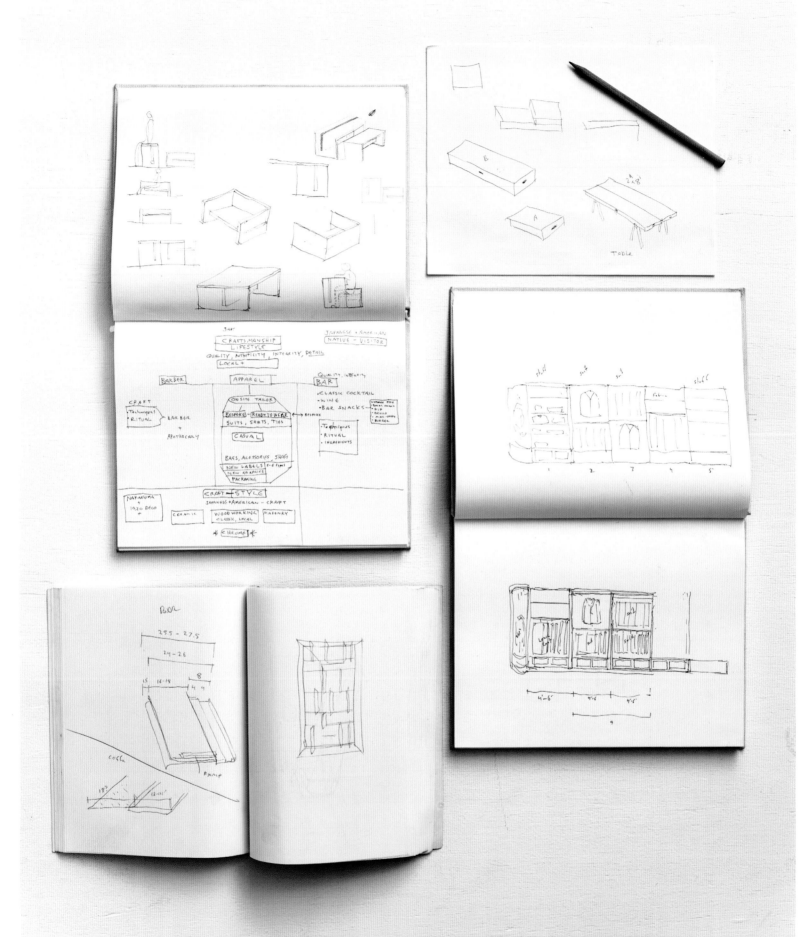

Introduction

People want to make big impressions: they want to do things on a grand scale. They try to create icons that end up on magazine covers, on social media. When they're designing a facade, they imagine how it will look from a distance, which is important, but it's just as important as how it looks up close. It's the difference between getting to know somebody through a photograph or the intimacy of a conversation. Up close is where lasting emotional impact is made.

When I was a student, the more I learned about design, the more I cared about the way things looked on a more intimate level. I wasn't interested in the panoramic view; I was thinking about being eighteen inches away from what we were working on, about being so near to it that I could feel it.

I've always been interested in design that activates the senses, that really touches you—the purely innate response. I'm attracted to the patina of brass, to worn stairs, to the smell of fire and burning rosemary. I try to design for the intersection between sense and place. That's why I'm attracted to design that feels familiar even when you can't explain why.

There's muscle memory, of course, but there's emotional memory too: how you felt as a kid when you went camping or smelled a favorite dish in the kitchen. Design can activate those memories, even if you're no longer conscious of them, tapping into a stored knowledge of sensual experiences that create innate responses—to surfaces, to the layout of a room, to its level of light. That's what I'm trying to design for, how things touch people in the most literal sense.

That's not exactly what I was taught at the University of Minnesota School of Architecture, where we dutifully studied Mies van der Rohe and his all-knowing perspective. But I was a good student, interested in the philosophy of design, history, and drawing. I did not do well in a class called Structures, which was just math and physics. It had none of the romance of design and was nonintuitive—and that just didn't appeal to me.

At that time, I was twenty-four, living in an old brick apartment building, within walking distance of the Walker Art Center, where I went almost every day. I also loved going to a restaurant called the Loring Café and Bar and went there almost every day too. The place impressed me—the crowd was diverse and creative, and there was always something different going on: you might see the owner gardening outside, dancers from a nearby troupe, or actors from a local theater company dropping in to perform. The Loring seemed to welcome and foster a cultivated chaos, and the atmosphere evolved as day became night, from a relaxed café where you could linger in the afternoon to an active bar. Sometimes there was live music—nothing ever seemed to be too planned—but everything the Loring staged was good. The level of taste was consistent—something you could trust—and that created a certain sense of community around the place itself. That had a strong effect on me.

When I was a full-time student, I worked twenty, sometimes even forty, hours a week at an architecture firm, Vincent James Associates Architects. In many ways, Vincent James was my first mentor. In addition to being an architect, he was also an artist. He made watercolors that I liked a lot and found quite moving. I was struck by their openness, how direct they were. He would make paintings as preparatory work, even though they could be very abstract. I admired his ongoing sense of curiosity.

Vincent was very interested in academic work and had a great sense of materiality—he was a believer in the haptic realm. In his office we designed in a very hands-on way. We'd build model after model; everybody in the office—even newcomers like me—did. When the firm won a prestigious commission to build a modernist house for a prominent Minneapolis family, I left school for a year to work on the project full-time. Working on this house—which had a facade made of limestone and glass walls that allowed light into the house throughout the day—I came into contact with many talented people from different fields, including George Hargreaves, then chairman of the Department of Landscape Architecture at the Harvard University Graduate School of Design, and artist and glass technologist James Carpenter.

Vince was very intuitive about how things should feel but also had a practical knowledge about how materials would age with use, and that important consideration has remained with me whenever I design a space. He also wasn't afraid to speak up in defense of how things would actually be used by the people who lived there. I learned to be wary of design flourishes that got attention but didn't really work. It was a reminder that our job wasn't finished when the construction was done and we photographed the house for our portfolio; that's when the life of the place was finally beginning. He was aware of seemingly prosaic details such as the driveway: he wanted to make sure that everything was as smooth as possible for the drivers coming and going, even if that meant using less-attractive pebbles.

Working on this house was not only the most immersive education I received but also a transformative experience. It was the first time I saw a project move from the drawing stage through construction, from theory to realization. I learned how crucial a builder's skill and experience are to the process of doing that. The project made me realize that I not only wanted to build things but also to see the project through from beginning to end, on location. I believed that for every architectural project I would go on to do after that, design and build would go hand in hand.

In 1998, I finished my thesis, which was about developing Chrystie Street in Lower Manhattan. I was interested in cultural programming, because that was a way to unify the neighborhoods. For me, bars, theaters, and restaurants are as important as the architecture itself; they impact a community. They're the living part of architecture.

At the time, the seven-block-long Sara D. Roosevelt Park, which runs from East Houston Street to Canal Street and between Chrystie and Forsyth Streets, served as a barrier between the more-gentrified Nolita neighborhood and the rastier Lower East Side. The thrust of the thesis was to stitch together the two neighborhoods by putting a movie theater with a public rooftop garden on Houston Street (this was before Sunshine Cinema had arrived), along with community meeting places, a restaurant complex, and an outdoor theater.

Of course, I had no idea that many years later I would open Freemans Restaurant just one block away from the site.

CHAPTER I

Freemans Restaurant

In 2001, I was working as the project architect on a new modernist restaurant in midtown Manhattan. Located in a well-known landmark building, the restaurant had a major contemporary art collection and a reputation for formality. The space was impressive, daunting, and very cold.

The designer we were working with was brilliant and famous, yet the project was adrift. We went over budget and drove the contractors crazy as we revised plans again and again. The designer's work became increasingly self-referential, moving away from addressing the experience of the people who were going to use the space every day: from the diners to the chefs and staff.

A few years later, the restaurant redid the entire room. The lesson was clear: when you cram perfect shapes— the shapes that architecture students are taught are fundamental to good design—into an old building, it doesn't add up. In a practical sense that's no surprise: with this particular building, the columns didn't line up. The front and back of the original room were inches off. In our precision, we designed everything according to the blueprint, down to a sixteenth of an inch, as is standard. Our design didn't fit into the space. We had to go back and shrink everything. It would have been comical if it didn't mean another two and a half years of work.

Above all, that project overlooked the fact that design has to start with human needs, and I believed it was time to change the model. I started to think about what sort of design could be based on imperfect, more unique shapes, to consider what would happen if we changed the geometry of the models around us. I began to look less at models and more at nature, like the ocean, a shape that is a closer metaphorical model to a lot of what happens in our lives. It's affected by storms, wind, and tides—it mirrors human emotions; it changes.

I started looking at gardens more closely. My mother loved gardens, and our house in rural Pennsylvania had wonderful ones. She often took me to Longwood Gardens, in Kennett Square. Spread over one thousand acres, the gardens—with their diverse layouts, various textures, and planting configurations—resonated and stayed with me.

As I began to consider these elaborate ecosystems in a new way, I started seeing more in them than a combination of plants, than a well-designed landscape: I saw compositions on an even grander scale that incorporated everything from the smallest insect to the moon. Instead of using a euclidean shape as my inspiration, I began to look at the evolution of ecosystems. An ecosystem is a form much in the same way that a room—from the lighting to the furniture to the art on the walls—is: they both read as a whole and create a mood. Change one element, and you have to consider the influence of that move on everything.

In architecture school, I was trained to draw plans and elevations—lines on paper—and students never thought about the effect that those lines would have on the people who ultimately stood within them. I didn't want to think about people in an abstract sense like that. Architectural training is not a bad education, but there is a danger that you're planning a house or a building at too far a remove from human needs. Rather than design from what felt to me like ten thousand feet in the air—with schematic drawings and cold blueprints—I wanted to become a part of the scene that I was designing for. When I began to work that way, I would forget I was even designing. It was design on an intimate scale. I would consider how things looked up close, whether they made people want to reach out and touch them. I kept asking myself how I could design for people. Yet I didn't have a big plan. I was against plans.

I draw every day and love it. I convert those drawings into schematic plans on computers. That's the language of architecture—you can't work without it. But the things I really respond to are all sensory. The way something feels, its texture, how it smells. That's why I love cooking, gardening, and old tweed coats. That's why I love woodworking and furniture that's made in a traditional way.

I began to think about what I came to call method design. I wanted to immerse myself in a project the way in which an actor immerses himself in a role that takes over his being. When I walked down Freemans Alley for the first time, I knew this was going to happen.

I discovered the space in October 2003 when I was looking for a location for a Halloween party. The leaves were changing; the days were getting shorter. The building was moody and brooding and gothic, like an Edgar Allan Poe story. It also reminded me of the colonial architecture of rural Pennsylvania where I grew up and where the historic buildings are wood-paneled, often painted, and spartan—not unlike Andrew Wyeth's interiors.

The space was singular—I knew right away that I wanted to open a restaurant there. I ditched the Halloween party idea, and the very next day I started to raise money for the restaurant. It was not the smoothest process. When I shared the news and plans for the space with my old friend Carlos Quirarte, he suggested I talk to an investor. I said I didn't know any investors. Carlos suggested I speak to William Tigertt, a friend we knew from Selvedge, a shop where I had sold ironic-slogan T-shirts that I had made.

I presented my business plan to Will and asked him if he knew anybody who might be interested in backing me. A few days later, he came back and said that he would. He is an expert on drinking, in a professional sense. He had the foresight, more than a decade ago, to see the return of a serious interest in cocktails. (Will has subsequently become an owner of Gothic Wine, a vineyard in Oregon.) We agreed that he would be responsible for the cocktail and wine program, while I would focus on interiors.

For Freemans Restaurant, I didn't draw a plan. I designed it using perspective drawings—thinking about the space cinematically from the point of view of the diner from the beginning to the end of the experience. In practice that meant thinking about what it felt like to approach Freemans. It meant walking down Freemans Alley—there's only one way to get to the restaurant—to arrive at a pair of wooden doors that open to reveal a hidden world, like an old tavern, with a zinc bar, wooden tables, taxidermy animal heads (now emblematic of the place), and painted paneled walls. That's how I envisioned people's progressive experience of the space, a natural experience that focused on sensory design.

At the time, restaurant interiors seemed very commercial, as if places to eat were shallow, interchangeable sets for food presentation. I wanted a place that felt real, like a home. I was trying to create a world I would be happy to live in. That was partly out of necessity and partly by design. I was a bit homesick and would spend hours studying books on Andrew Wyeth in my bedroom. I always loved the starkness of his interiors, a white wall with a crack, a ceiling with an iron hook, a paned window looking out on a dry winter field and a young brown calf. The muted colors—a loden jacket against brown bark, the gray of a stormy sky, the pale taupe of dry grass— appealed to me. The paintings reminded me not only of my childhood but also of the era in which I grew up, evoking cultural memories, and I hoped that the things that moved me would move other people.

In designing Freemans, I considered how the failed midtown restaurant project was designed in a vacuum. It didn't matter if the cuisine was Japanese, French, or Italian. We were supposed to deliver the design and consider the food later. At Freemans I wanted to design everything at the same time—the food, the flowers, the lighting. I even wrote a simple narrative about the restaurant, portraying it as a clandestine tavern during the Revolutionary War, a meeting of the Old World and the New. I wanted it to be inspired by American traditions, yet specifically a New York place, a place that couldn't exist anywhere else.

When we were coming up with the menu, we chose dishes that were in sync with the setting: traditional American food, the comfort food from childhood—beef stew, mashed potatoes, grilled steak, and chowder—the sorts of dishes you'd find in an old classic cookbook like *The Joy of Cooking*. We wanted to offer a menu that was familiar enough to people—steak and potatoes, brook trout, bananas Foster—that it might trigger memories of a fond time in their lives. My father had cooked like this, and I will always remember him grilling an entire fish whenever we camped. Our artichoke dip, by the way, is from the Loring, my favorite restaurant from my student days in Minneapolis—and it's not a secret recipe but right on the side of a Hellmann's mayonnaise jar.

We opened in September 2004, less than a year after that October meeting. Not everything was smooth at first: we had two hot plates but no burners, no ovens, no air-conditioning, and no heat. We had no host—I seated people myself for the first month. We almost didn't have any silverware either. Our first chef, Chloe Osborne, and I bought some in Chinatown the afternoon we opened. Chloe was feeling the pressure of the moment—with good reason—and while we were in a cab with bags of knives and forks, she said, "You have no idea what you're getting yourself into, do you?" She was right. But if I had known, if I had analyzed the viability of creating and running a successful restaurant in a rational way, I may have never done it in the first place. I had never worked in a restaurant and knew nothing about running one.

When we first opened, people couldn't always find Freemans Alley—friends thought I was crazy to open a restaurant that far from the street—sometimes they still can't, even with smartphone maps. I was concerned that if Freemans failed, people would say it was because it was too far off the beaten path, at the end of a narrow alley. But walking down Freemans Alley is now a crucial part of the experience—you feel like you're strolling in a forgotten part of the city.

Fortunately, the restaurant became a success very quickly. Soon we were able to add the things that restaurants need—a professional kitchen, good ventilation, a walk-in refrigerator—things that were mostly invisible to diners. What they noticed and what drove the place, and still does, is the sense of theater.

Running a restaurant is not unlike the production of a play. There is the preparation, the routines that are repeated day after day, and then, of course, the production every night. The staff prepares for the performances, lighting candles and setting tables. The kitchen is the orchestra, well rehearsed. The diners are patrons and players all at once; they observe and are observed. The evenings typically have many acts. Cocktails at 6:00 P.M., early diners, then the crush. Late at night people kiss and get drunk and break dishes and we clean it up and do it again.

I look at Freemans and the other restaurants I am involved with as evolving spaces. They're never finished. I like to add pictures, books, and furniture, just like I do at home. Over the years at Freemans, we've brought in a lot more taxidermy, more tables, and more paintings. If I see something at an antique store, I'll buy it if it just feels right—and worry about where I'm going to put it later. Doing that keeps the project alive even when you're not there. You buy a great chair, trusting it'll find a home, and it does, and then you can't imagine the space any other way.

The exterior of doors of the restaurant as well as their vivid blue color were inspired from a trip to Paris many years ago. Everywhere I went, I seemed to notice these great painted doors that led into the courtyards of apartment buildings. Sometimes the doors were so big that they had a smaller door within them, which was what people actually used. The doors impressed me because they were well considered, both functionally and aesthetically.

I wanted to have doors at Freemans, too, rather than the usual nondescript but practical roll-down gate, and I chose the blue because the color stands out at the end of the gray alley. And I was obsessed with getting the color just right. I had a book with a blue spine that really stood out on the shelf and I tried to match it. I would paint part of the door and would walk down the alley to make sure the color was visible enough. After a few tries I got the blue right, and the doors are now an iconic element of the restaurant.

We didn't hire professional carpenters to build Freemans; we did it ourselves. Our corners weren't perfect, not everything aligned. We used very inexpensive materials from the lumberyard next door. We painted all the walls, which aligned nicely with the colonial vibe, as walls were often painted during that time.

Paint and a strategic placement of caulk allowed us to camouflage a certain shortcoming in our craftsmanship. We used a lot of white, pale yellow, and black because these colors are generally inexpensive and, more important, aesthetically neutral. I mixed the green, which has become a signature of the restaurant, myself. Later on, a friend asked if it was a color from Farrow & Ball, the legendary English paint company. At the time, I hadn't even heard of them, but I wished I had: getting that green just right took quite a lot of time.

When I began to decorate Freemans, I bought taxidermy heads of a white-tailed deer and a black boar on something of a whim. I guess I was looking for something that felt like the opposite of the city and also reminded me of where I grew up, Chadds Ford, Pennsylvania, which meant a lot to me, and expressed a strong aspect of my vision of what I wanted Freemans to be—a place that evoked a sense of history, of people coming there regularly over many years, of having pride in its roots from an earlier, simpler, more rustic time.

Ultimately, we brought a lot of taxidermy into Freemans. When we opened, taxidermy wasn't used much in restaurant environments, but we liked it and kept buying more of it. Today people associate taxidermy with us, and it's also become a popular fixture in bars and restaurants all over town.

CHAPTER 2

Freemans Sporting Club

In 2005, the restaurant expanded to include a second room, with more tables and an additional bar. People could—and would—drink during the long waits for tables. We expanded to the upper floor too. At first we had an office, a very informal one, which we created by putting in a large canvas military tent along with a few tables and some Oriental rugs. Then we had another room and two private dining rooms. Freemans felt like an entire world. It was time to buy more taxidermy.

I also bought a pool table from a guy in New Jersey who sold it to me for a dollar because I agreed to come over and take it out of his garage. Friends would come by the restaurant after work, even late at night, to play pool and drink wine. Every now and then we would head out to the country and shoot skeet, fly-fish, and camp too.

It was very casual, but it was also a conscious effort to stay connected, as our careers and personal lives were getting increasingly busy. These planned excursions were an effort to keep us together; otherwise, we'd never see one another. We just liked going on informal road trips, being outside, and misbehaving. The restaurant staff began to call us the Freemans Sporting Club.

At that time, I was wearing a lot of suits from the 1950s that I bought at thrift stores. The suits never fit me quite right though—they were all too small; men were just built differently then. I also liked old deadstock fabrics that were heavy with a great sense of texture—things like English tweed, mohair, corduroy, and wool. The fabrics were rough, sturdy, and didn't wrinkle; I loved the way they aged when I wore them a lot. The aesthetic was the opposite of smooth cashmere fabrics often found at designer boutiques, which I didn't really like, and I was tired of streetwear.

In 2005, about a year after we opened the restaurant, a retail space became available up on Rivington Street, at the mouth of Freemans Alley. We took the space, first to control the entrance to the restaurant—we didn't want a bank to go in there. We had a fledgling custom-suit business we were running above the restaurant, selling mostly to friends, that we figured we'd move down to the new retail store. At the time, before the menswear revolution—before MR PORTER, blogs, and Instagram—I wasn't a big shopper. Most men aren't; once men find a brand that works, they stick with it—sometimes for decades—out of efficiency, reliability, and habit. I wanted to make a store for myself, a place men I knew would shop and feel comfortable, a place that would also appeal to a downtown crowd. I wanted to create a brand that was dependable and make pieces that could be new heirlooms, like those I was finding in flea markets and thrift shops. We thought of the store as a sutlery—the term for an outfitter that stocks an army before an expedition—and we called it Freemans Sporting Club.

Like most men, my business partner Kent Kilroe and I don't dress in seasons, so our goal was to make clothes guys wear all the time and can wear all year round— a gray wool suit, blue jeans, chambray shirts. In a way, the store was antifashion. We took the long view: we weren't trying to make the next thing; we were trying to make clothing you would never get rid of.

Our suits were made by Martin Greenfield, the legendary Brooklyn clothier, whose name I got from an old man who sold me the deadstock fabric I used for all my suits. Martin Greenfield loved those old fabrics, and he agreed to make a small run of suits for us. Just as we used local bakers, fishermen, and farmers to supply our food, we hired some of the city's best tailors to help make, refine, and alter our clothes. We even made on-site bespoke clothing based on paper patterns.

We found more deadstock flannel fabrics and had a shirtmaker in midtown make plaid shirts. They were made largely by hand, and because they were crafted from vintage fabric, they had a natural old-world quality.

Much of the clothing we made came out of simple need, that is, things we wanted to wear but were hard to find, like good chinos. I wanted chinos that were cut like jeans, closer to the leg, and fit lower on the waist, so we decided to make a pair in olive green and another in khaki. We called them Winchesters. They've become best sellers for us, and we now make them every season, in all colors and fabrics.

Not everything we made was practical. Sometimes we even veered toward the more rarified. An oversize, double-breasted, navy melton wool overcoat worn by Andrew Wyeth in a wonderful Bruce Weber photograph inspired one of our coats, which we called the Revere Coat, due to its Revolutionary War vibe. More formal than a peacoat, but longer and with a bigger collar, it looked like something you could wear into a tavern in the eighteenth century. Martin Greenfield's tailors made a handful of them for us. The coats were very striking, but they were expensive to produce, so we made only a few. I wish we'd made more, actually, because people still come into the store and ask for them.

When we started making suits, we wanted them to have an expressive quality. We made them in heavy and unusual fabrics that made people want to touch them. They looked like something you might have inherited from an interesting uncle or found at a smart British thrift store. They certainly didn't look new. That's what we wanted: to make clothing with a sense of history, a sense of how it was made, and, just like

Freemans Restaurant, something that alluded to the craftsmen who built it.

In the back of the store we built a barbershop. At that time, a man could go to an elaborate salon, which never felt right, or the local barber, which was a nice experience but too often resulted in a schoolboy haircut. My partners Sam Buffa and William Tigertt and I wanted to create a space where you could get a straight-razor shave and a no-nonsense cut. We also wanted a place that had a strong sense of the neighborhood it was in.

A relationship with a barber is very specific: you see him every couple of weeks, you talk to him about what you're up to, and, of course, he has an impact on your appearance. All of which is to say: once you settle on a good one, like a mechanic or a tailor, he's a part of your life. Because there's a specific social element to a barbershop—in a way it's like a bar—we wanted barbers who weren't just talented, but were social too. There's always a hum of conversation in a barbershop and we wanted to capture that for a group of younger men. But it wasn't hard to find young barbers, from the East Village to Brighton Beach; they were thrilled to work at a shop where there was such good energy.

We carried the products that we loved to use: shaving cream from Italy (Proraso), toothpaste from France (Botot), cologne made in a monastery outside Florence (Santa Maria Novella), pine-scented soap (Lightfoot's). We didn't take appointments—it was first come, first serve. The waits were so long we added a reservation system so people could book up to a month in advance, down to the minute (a little technology has improved the experience), and expanded into a larger space next door to the clothing store.

Together, the men's store and barbershop created the kind of place we wanted to spend time. We played the music we wanted to hear, sold old copies of *Playboy* we liked reading, hired salesmen who were our friends. It didn't seem like a radical idea, but there was nothing else like it. The concept was a huge success: since then we've been widely imitated; barbershops like this have opened all over the country.

People have strong feelings about denim. When I moved to New York, I was friends with some denim-obsessives who gave me a hard time because I wasn't educated in the ways of the short loom. They thought about denim all the time and constantly looked for ways to improve it, even sanding "whisper marks" onto their jeans.

I never became as intense as they were; I didn't want to devote that much time to upkeep. But making the perfect pair of jeans—one of the holy grails of men's fashion—did become an obsession at Freemans. We made a pilgrimage to find cone denim from Kentucky and tracked down remarkable Japanese selvage denim too. We experimented with different fits and cuts and constantly tried to perfect them. There's something about denim that can make you lose your rationality. All my related experiments made perfect sense at the time—even wearing them in the shower to handwash them.

Finding good barber chairs is not as easy as you'd think—especially if you want vintage ones. Tracking them down involved a lot of research and time on the road. Co-owners and barbers Miles Martinez and Ruben Aronov searched for them in garages, storage units, and barber shops in Brooklyn and Queens, and even drove long hours to Pennsylvania, Delaware, North Carolina, and Canada. In the end, we found seven chairs—each of which weighs about two hundred pounds—manufactured by Takara Belmont in Japan in the late 1950s and early 1960s and imported to the United States.

We see the chairs as classic now, but at the time they were made they were considered novel, even futuristic, as their design was influenced by the space race. We had the metal refinished, and the headrests and seats re-covered with leather from the Horween Leather Company, a business that's been making high-quality goods in Chicago since 1905. The chairs are timeless—like a lot of things we like at Freemans—and we think they'll still look good decades from now.

Men are creatures of habit. When we find something that works we stick with it. We like efficiency and ease. We respond to things that are dependable. We don't need a couple of the next best thing, we need the one good thing. That's one reason that men are loyal to their barbers. They like the routine of seeing the same person every few weeks. Most men get their hair cut to maintain what they like, which is why they like to know their barber well.

Add to the routine the ongoing conversations a guy has with his barber—about travel, about work, about dating. They're a reassuring part of life. The barber does his job well and remembers you and what you like. It's a welcome relationship that every man I know values.

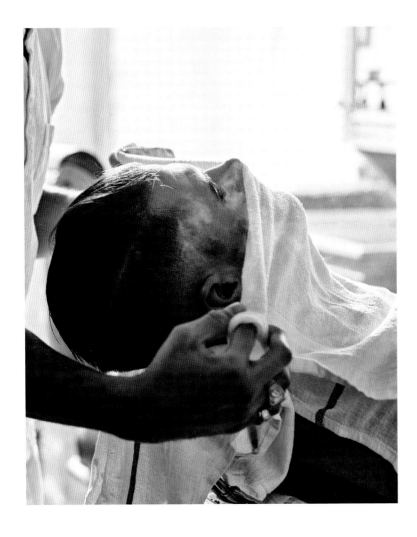
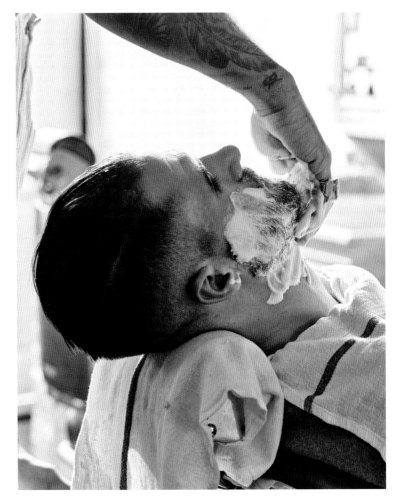
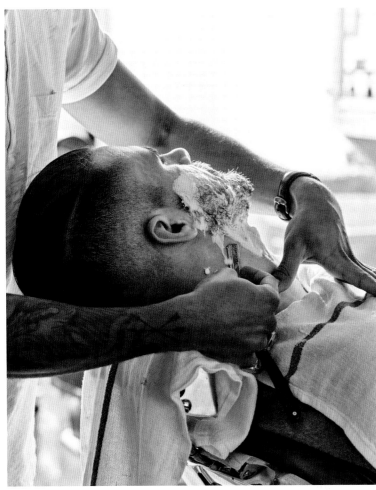
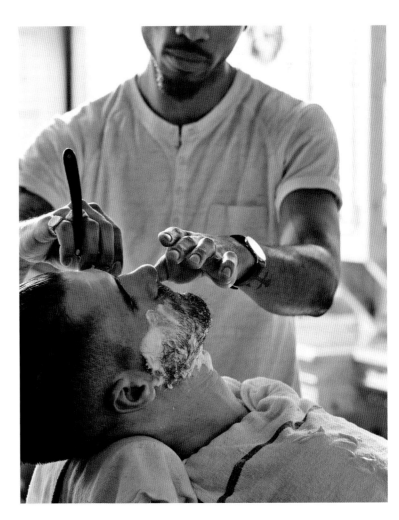

FREEMANS
SPORTING
CLUB

EST. 2005

CHAPTER 3

Total Design in Tokyo

When we had a chance to bring Freemans Sporting Club to Tokyo, it was an opportunity to design a five-story building and to create a new vision of the entire Freemans world. The plan was to create a bar and café on the lowest level, a sportswear area on the ground floor, tailored clothing with a tailoring studio on the second floor, and a barbershop on the third floor.

While Freemans in New York expanded horizontally from restaurant to clothier to barbershop over the years, the plan for Tokyo was to build Freemans vertically in eight months. The contractors couldn't speak English, and I couldn't speak Japanese, but we communicated through drawings and passed construction samples back and forth. I also traveled to Tokyo at least ten times during the design-and-build process.

Tokyo is an inspiring place—the people embrace design; they try to understand your vision. They consider the aesthetics of all things—whether they're presenting food, weaving mats, or sweeping a pathway in a park. The Japanese reputation for impeccability and precision is based in truth: the people we worked with on the Tokyo store were all experts who knew their craft and did everything with great care.

The Freemans' aesthetic and its incarnations are meant to work together, to complement each other. Instead of an alley—which brought together the restaurant, clothing shop, and barbershop in New York—we chose to treat the space more like an ecosystem or garden. To create a more natural integration, we unified this single vertical space with a garden wall.

With its nondescript, flat gray concrete structure and aluminum and glass windows, the exterior of the original building looked like a brutalist parking garage or, actually, the failed hair salon that the space had been. As the new home of Freemans Sporting Club, it was a far cry from the brownstones and residential scale of Manhattan's Lower East Side. I was hoping to make the exterior more evocative of Freemans New York by adding an elaborately weathered stone facade. Something got lost in translation though, because it wasn't until construction was under way that we discovered that we had to keep the front of the building as it was. I broke into a panic—the incongruity between the exterior and the interior was a big issue for me. The interior spaces were quite intimate, and while they were clean, they weren't antiseptic at all. I didn't want to have these warm rooms housed in a cold white box.

Fortunately, I remembered a time when I had visited the Louvre during a large-scale renovation; the museum had installed a scrim with a photograph of the building printed on it over the scaffolding. Inspired by that, I made a Photoshop rendering of a brownstone and had it printed on a scrim that now floats on a bar infrastructure that hangs in front of the building. In a city that has rebuilt itself so many times, the treatment makes sense. It has a postmodern effect, and, just as important, it lets light in.

Another sticking point was the stairway that connects all the floors—it was a little sterile. To my surprise, it was hard to find an Oriental rug in Japan. So I went to a carpet liquidator in Paramus, New Jersey, and purchased enough linear feet of carpet to cover the entire floor, and had it all shipped to Tokyo. The idea for the barbershop was to make it a heightened reference to the New York space. One of the most dominant materials in the shop is the subway tile, which is used on the floor, but is impossible to find in Tokyo. Again we went to a New Jersey supplier and had the tile shipped to Japan.

We also included a hand-built, six-foot-long aquarium, which sits in the middle of the barbershop, as a nod to the barber I went to when I was a kid. A Vietnam vet who rode a Harley-Davidson, he made a real impression on me. In his shop he had a fish tank with a single trout—about two feet long—that he'd caught but that had outgrown the tank, so it had to swim in place. In keeping with the cultural attention to detail, my Japanese partners sent me countless photographs of fish, along with their length in centimeters, to choose from. This amused me, since they were all very, very small and looked almost exactly the same. I had imagined re-creating the fish tank oddity of my childhood with another two-foot-long trout, or maybe an octopus or a turtle. There are hundreds of fish the size of a gyoza instead, but everybody loves that aquarium.

The Vans-Freemans Sporting Club collaboration was the result of a surprising turn of improvisation in the Tokyo shop. My Japanese partners approached Vans about doing slip-on sneakers with the red-and-white motif on the front door of the barbershop, which also matches the business cards and matchbooks that we made for the barbers in New York and Tokyo. They presented the designs, which also included a custom shoebox with the same striped pattern, and we were thrilled. They sold out of them immediately. We didn't sell the sneakers in the United States, although a few pairs made their way to Rivington Street and onto barbers' feet.

When we were considering what music to play in the Tokyo store, there was a series of emails and meetings which set out to decide just that. Should it be different on different floors, so somebody buying a pair of jeans would hear something more lively than a man buying a suit? What about the barbershop? What about the bar?

I liked the idea of having the music be appropriate to each area, but wanted to leave it to our partners to interpret, particularly as one of them was a DJ with an extensive record collection, and I trusted his taste. Our partners couldn't dream of deciding all of this, though. They wanted me to give them our exact playlist from New York, to insure the experience was authentic. With a little help from our most music-savvy New York employees we assembled and sent along specific playlists, from the barbershop, the men's store, and the restaurant.

At the Tokyo store opening months later, everything was perfect: the merchandising, lighting, floors, and the music. They had successfully re-created the details of our New York store, but that should never have come as a surprise.

In the course of renovating the Tokyo building it became clear that there was an unfortunate view from large windows on every single floor onto a six-story concrete wall. It was a giant void that looked like a brutalist missile silo, and we knew we had to do something about it. We thought about painting it or installing hanging lights or objects, none of which really had any appeal.

Then I had an idea to create a hanging garden, a living wall. This six-story wall was open to the elements, so it made sense, and it seemed in keeping with the Japanese love of creating a precisely delineated, well-tended garden. Our Japanese partners embraced the idea and carried it off in the most thoughtful and thorough way, hiring an expert gardener to oversee its care. Now there's a warm view from every place in the building.

After the success of Freemans, we had offers to expand the business across the city, even the country. But that didn't hold much appeal; I didn't want to remake the same thing in another place. I wanted to move on, to think about other projects with different aesthetics. I'm a restless designer in general; I want to try new things, get into a new era—the same way I would get into a new band or a certain genre of film when I was younger. I wanted to build something that referred to a different era than Freemans did. You can seek things out, but, sometimes, the right project has a way of finding you.

CHAPTER 4

The World at Large

THE RUSTY KNOT

The Rusty Knot came about by happy accident. Unlike Freemans, which is hidden at the end of an alley, the Rusty Knot is on the West Side Highway at the end of West Eleventh Street. I actually met my partner in the business, Ken Friedman, for the first time in the space itself, then a defunct bar. Connected through a friend, we agreed to meet to discuss whether we might want to work together and to check out the location at the same time. I immediately responded to his energy and sense of humor, and when he said that he thought the dive would be a good place to open a bar—just a couple blocks from the Spotted Pig, another restaurant of his—I was in.

We wanted to make a place that was an easygoing late-night hangout, so we decided to open a dive bar. I've always loved dives, from my time in Minneapolis, a city blessed with many of them, and in New York—though more and more of them are closing. Of course, nobody sets out to open a dive bar. A bar becomes a dive over many, many years. But we wanted to open one that felt like it already had the veneer of age and would just get better with time. People would come into a bar that already felt decades old. What became the Rusty Knot would require the opposite of maintenance—the older and more beat-up it felt, the better.

We built plywood booths that people started to carve their initials in—which I loved. There were red leather chairs with cane armrests, old wooden boats, hanging buoys, maritime paintings, some photographs of actors from the 1970s that we autographed ourselves to make it seem as if they had been regulars. One of the first things I bought was a vintage ice maker. It's just right for an old bar. It has a simple, no-nonsense, functional design that is very satisfying—and it works well too.

While Freemans felt like a secret, the Rusty Knot was right out in the open. You can see boats and the light on the Hudson River. You can also see the sunset. The place makes you feel like you're in the Florida Keys. The jukebox is free and plays yacht rock. A game of pool costs a quarter.

Freemans has a rigorous, classic cocktail program, where everything is precisely measured, but the Rusty

Knot is built for speed. We serve spiced coladas out of ceramic coconuts and adorn the cocktails with colorful paper umbrellas and plastic mermaids. The beer is cheap, the wine, from a box. We use unbreakable red plastic cups. There's a sense of familiarity, the cups remind people of pizzerias they went to as teenagers.

The weekend we opened, in 2008, the bar was more crowded than we thought it would be. Ken and I texted everybody we knew, and somehow they all showed up. We were not just over capacity—the place legally holds seventy-four people—we were double that. We ran out of liquor. We ran out of everything. We had to close for two days. But the Knot, as we call it, was never meant to be a hot spot. And though we've had all sorts of parties there, and DJs, and a short-lived party bus that picked up people in Williamsburg and drove them to our door— it has settled down into a neighborhood place where I go for a relaxing drink with friends, which is just what we meant for it to be.

When we were building the Rusty Knot, I wanted the music on our jukebox, which has always been free, to be as unique to the bar as possible—an unexpected late 1970s–early 1980s soundtrack, with musicians like Christopher Cross, Todd Rundgren, Loggins & Messina, Thin Lizzy, Spooky Tooth, Savoy Brown, Flying Burrito Brothers, Leon Russell, Flower Traveling Band, Uriah Heap, Michael McDonald, and Gene Clark. Yacht rock, before there was a name for it. Friends would ask if we could play The Smiths or Blondie. I would say, "No way! Don't you get the theme of this bar?"

I guess I took my mission to an extreme. One night, I tried to play a certain song, but it just wouldn't come on the jukebox. Later I understood why: the bartenders had figured out a way to lock out certain songs that they just couldn't stand hearing one more time. So I gave up on enforcing the playlist: sometimes you have to let a place evolve, and if people want Blondie, you give it to them.

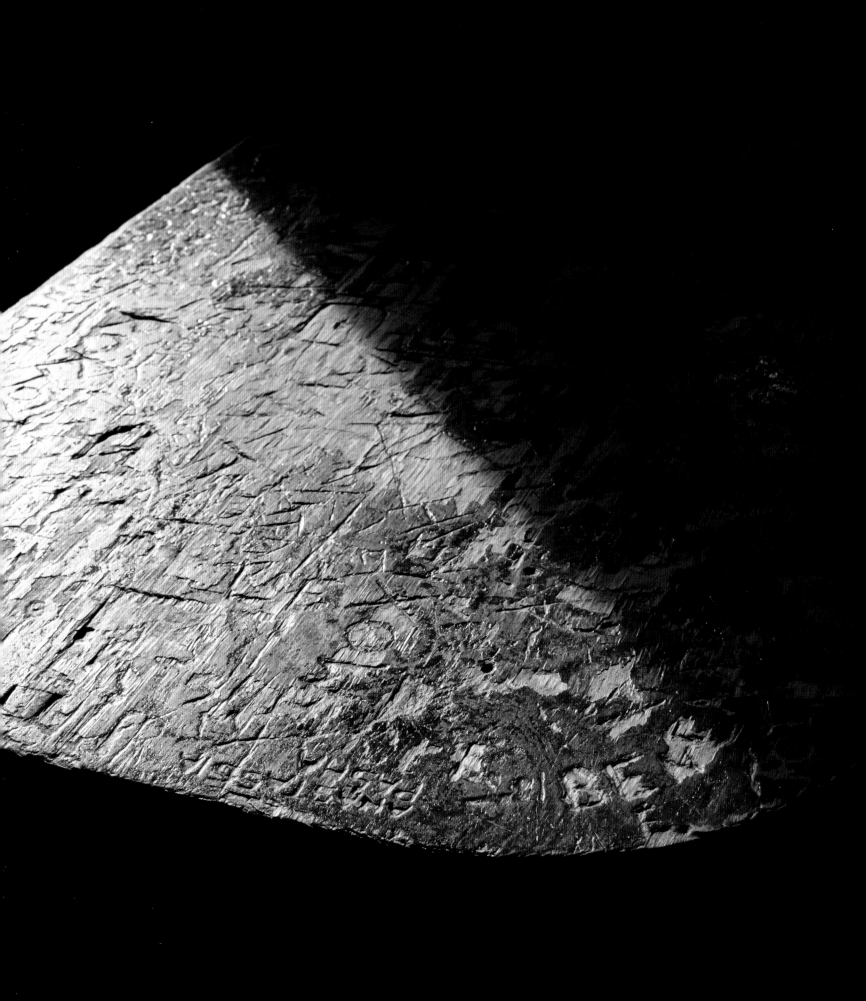

Incorporating a sense of memory into the design process is important to me. That can be an elevated concept, but sometimes it's straightforward, like in the case of the Rusty Knot, where I incorporated a bit of the vibe of the basement rec room of one of my very good friends from my teenage years. That room had a linoleum floor, a jukebox, and a pool table; we used to lift weights, listen to Led Zeppelin, and play pool. And actually, my friend's father had re-created it to bring elements of his childhood into his adult life.

For the Rusty Knot, we drew on that space, bringing in the pool table and the jukebox, and it turned out that those very things seemed to remind people of their childhood or a place from their past too. I've found that my memories of a place can evolve into a design in an honest way that conjures similar memories in other people; the space expresses the authenticity. If you try too hard, the result is contrived.

ISA

The Rusty Knot was a small project; there was no real kitchen to speak of. It worked despite its lack of ambition—or perhaps because of it. The next restaurant I worked on would require more intensive work. I found the space by chance. I was sitting in a car in Williamsburg, waiting with a friend for a real estate broker. When I pointed out the boarded-up building across the street that had a For Rent sign on it, my friend said that it was a garage he was trying to rent for parking. I had always wanted to open a restaurant in Brooklyn, and the space looked promising.

The landlord reminded me of a Texas rancher, with a ten-gallon hat, cowboy boots, and, as clichéd as it sounds, a bowlegged walk. His name was John, but he called himself Joe Hammer. We talked for half an hour at his desk, an empty pizza box set on a metal drum of paint, then made a deal. It was one of the simplest, most satisfying transactions I've ever had.

While designing ISA, I became a father for the first time, and while waiting for the baby, I thought about my own dad a lot. I have always admired the fact that my parents designed and built our home—my father made the tables, the sofa, and the stereo speakers; my mother baked bread and tended the garden. I saw making ISA as a way to return to working by hand, like my parents did. The restaurant's name is an homage to them somewhat; *isa* is the Estonian word for "father."

It took two years to design and build ISA, and I was immersed in the project in every way. We made everything by hand on-site: the floors, walls, and ceilings; the tables, the bar top, stools, benches, and shelves; even the lighting. We used reclaimed materials found within one hundred miles of the restaurant. The ceiling beams came from the Brooklyn Navy Yard, the wood slabs from upstate New York.

When I was designing, I looked a lot at 1970s West Coast culture. I was interested in people who had moved off the grid, who lived in geodesic domes, who were self-reliant. I looked at the *Whole Earth Catalog*, particularly the people in it; they reminded me of people I knew, people who responded to the locavore movement, who made beer, who made pottery. Something in me was reacting against the detachment of the computer, like I wanted to reach back into the past and bring my parents' interests from the 1970s into the present. When I was a kid, a friend's father told me that when I grew up I would turn into my dad, that we all do that. I insisted, as most kids would have, that there was no way that would happen. But as you get older, of course, and especially if you have kids, you realize just how much you have in common with your parents. As much as you want to make your own way, you recognize the deeper connection, and that's something that I embraced during this project, that this work could be personal, that it could represent the sensibility I grew up with. Letting that happen was something new for me; it was almost cathartic.

The chef, Ignacio Mattos, was as hands-on as everybody else. He worked closely with our construction team to build the restaurant, helping to install the ceiling and to sand down tables—particularly the fourteen-foot-long kitchen table—and he even helped carry in the heavy marble top. Ignacio had worked at Il Buco, where I had admired his cooking, and he had worked with the great Argentine chef Francis Mallmann, who was renowned for cooking over fire. I went to Uruguay and Argentina with Ignacio to tour the restaurants where Mallmann had worked, to check out the cooks' methods and to take in the ambience of those places.

Ultimately, ISA's menu was inspired by the experimental nature of building the restaurant. When we opened in 2011, we served dishes such as sardine skeletons, incredible beef tartare with sunchoke puree, and a gnudi with four cheeses that was the best pasta dish I've ever eaten. We were nominated for a James Beard Award our first year in business. The intense creativity Ignacio pushed for in the kitchen and I had pushed for in the design of the space made for an amazing time of experimentation. An incredible coincidence in all of this was that my first child, my daughter Tessa, was born the same day as Ignacio's first, his son Paco. I look back on that time with Ignacio fondly, and I carry what I learned from him with me in all the projects I do.

When we take over a space for a restaurant, my view is that we're contributing to an ongoing history. We're adding to the story of the space, but we want to respect what's come before. I look closely at what's already there and consider how to use it—whether to add complexity or contradiction. Again, I like there to be a sense of imperfection, of open-endedness. When something isn't quite finished it's more human.

At ISA, we enlarged a door to make an opening to connect the bar to the dining room. But we left part of the wall and the white finish just the way it was. At my house in upstate New York, we renovated our kitchen, but left the brick wall and painted it white, which was a nice reference to the history of the house. There are walls by the front bar in Freemans that are original too. There's often an instinct to finish things off, to make them much more polished, but sometimes leaving objects and structures the way they're found serves them and the space best.

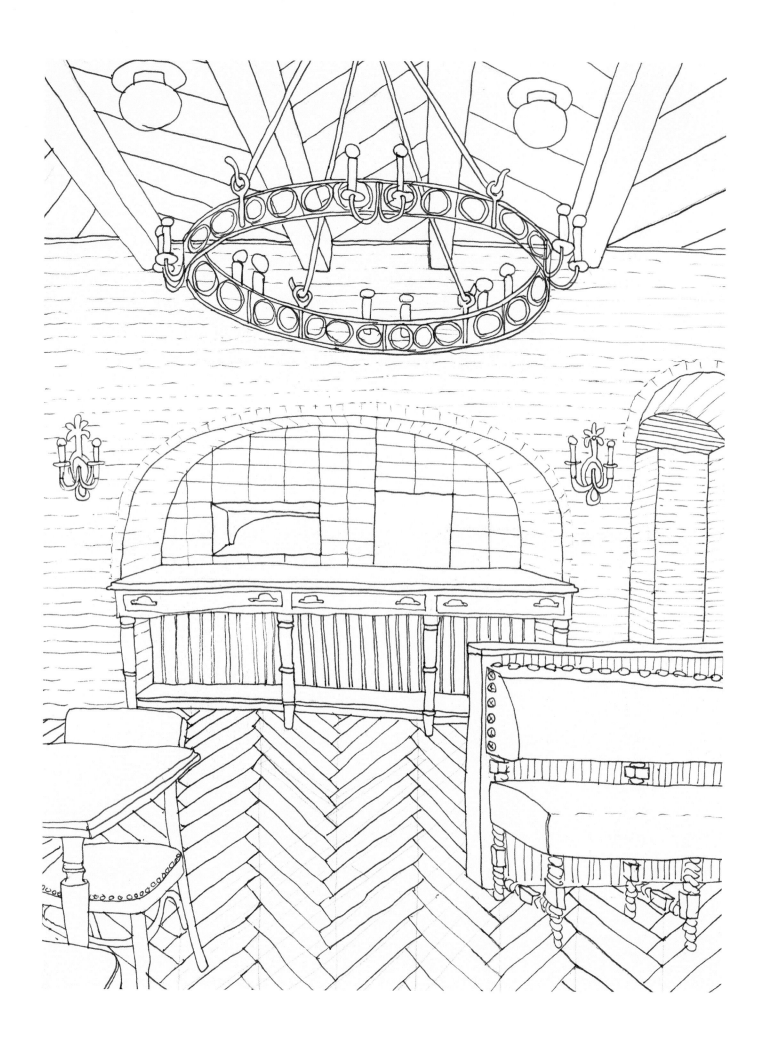

GEMMA

In 2007, restaurateur Serge Becker introduced me to Sean McPherson and Eric Goode, the talented duo behind many great New York restaurants and bars. They were working on the Bowery Hotel, and they asked me to design the restaurant in the unfinished hotel. The only thing they insisted on was that it be Italian.

The building had once been a dormitory at New York University, and the restaurant was being built in what was the parking garage—it was a space with nothing around it. So we had to build the walls, which I then thought of as a shell in which we had to include the classic elements of an Italian restaurant: ceramic tile floor, painted white brick, and wood beam ceilings. These were the backdrops that represented a certain sensibility and, because they were natural materials, would all age well.

I stained the oak-paneled walls myself. When it came to decorating the room, we searched for antiques that expressed good taste with a little bit of playfulness thrown into the mix. We wanted the room to evoke a sense of history, but also to communicate the Italian personality. We included everything from wicker cases that would hold Chianti bottles (which we knew were practically a cliché) to exotic African sculptures (which were completely unexpected), to reassuring antique landscape paintings.

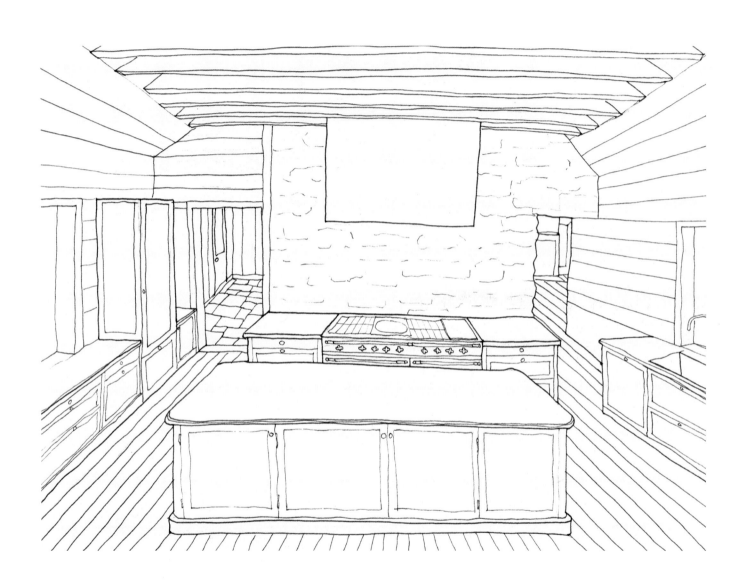

CHAPTER 5

A Home Upstate

When my wife, Courtney, and I were dating, during the week we lived in the same building as Freemans, a few floors above the restaurant. On the weekends we'd rent random houses in upstate New York. A few years later, when I was looking to buy a stone house, like those I had known growing up, I looked in the areas we had stayed.

After visiting at twenty or thirty houses over many weeks, we came to a house with a swing and a rocking bench that overlooked a pond. As soon as I saw the place, I knew I wanted to grow old there. Everything about the house and grounds—the stone walls, the wood-beamed ceiling, the wide plank floors, the four huge white pine trees in the backyard that supported a hammock, the fieldstone walls that divide the fields and woods on the property, even the pine needles on the ground, reminded me of my past yet spoke to the future. For the first time, I thought of marriage, of kids, of aging, of continuity, I could picture our lives unfolding there.

Built in the late eighteenth century, the house is set back from the main road, on a ridge that looks down across a valley and over to Mohonk Mountain. The driveway is a former logging road abandoned long ago. There's a constant breeze on the property, which I love; it feels poetic to me somehow. I talk about it so much that my wife makes fun of me.

Everything about the house is slightly crooked, but its imperfections appeal to my sense of what I've always liked about design in the world. I want to contribute to it in a way that is equally imperfect. The place feels relaxed. The house itself is modest; it has five rooms. The first floor has a main bedroom and a big living room with low, beamed ceilings and a sizable fireplace. There's a small upstairs bedroom that we divided into two rooms, connected by a loft, for our daughters. Eventually, we added a kitchen and a mudroom.

When we first got into the house, there were a lot of things we wanted to change. But we started outdoors and lived with the house as it was. We never wanted to touch the original structure, and the changes we made were gradual. It's good to sit with something and not rush into changing it.

At first, I was obsessed with landscaping. For four years, we cleared fields and wooded areas. We opened up the land around the house itself. I also planted and put in boxwood hedges along the edge of the yard, because I love how they smell in the fall, how they look in the snow. Boxwood also recalls early American history for me, as it's in abundance in colonial Williamsburg and planted near Independence Hall in Philadelphia. We became friendly with the owner of a small antiques store in town, and many of his pieces ended up in our house—and at Freemans too.

Over time we began to make some changes. The original house has low, seven-foot ceilings and tiny windows—it's a winter space. We added a kitchen that's the opposite of that: bright and airy, and with a high ceiling, it's designed for summer. All the doors open to the outdoors, and the windows are across from one another so I can catch my beloved breeze.

A house should be functional. We thought about what we wanted to do—cooking, playing with our daughters, swimming, or sitting outside with a glass of wine and looking at the view—then we tried to arrange our house so all these things could be done as simply as possible and to encourage everyone to spend time outside.

Now the house is a huge part of our lives. We look forward to heading out of town each week. We have our routine: we pack the girls in the car, try to beat traffic out of town, and open a bottle of wine when we arrive. It's incredible how you can discover a place partly by chance, and it becomes a focal point for everything you do.

I love breakfast. I usually wake up around 5:30 or 6:00 A.M., even on the week-ends, with my youngest daughter, Isla. She sets up her spot for her meal on our big chair by the fireplace. I make a pot of coffee and toast with jam and lots of butter. She typically scrapes the butter and jam off the bread with her teeth and asks for more.

I love watching the light change as the sun rises, the deer in the field, the fog on the pond, and the robins as they dart around, stop suddenly to look for worms in spring, then dart around again. If it's not too cold, we like to go outside in our pajamas and rain boots in the early morning chill to smell the air.

When they're young, most boys imagine a day when they'll have grown up and be a man who knows everything, who suddenly has all the answers the way they believe their dads do. Over time, though, they realize their fathers were not perfect, that they had insecurities and shortcomings—and that it's okay that they do. In other words, they accept their fathers' humanity.

That was certainly true for me. When I became a father, I realized that being a good parent isn't about having all the answers or being right—it's more important to provide a sense of security, comfort, and safety for your kids. I try to establish ways of living and habits, as well as rituals and traditions, that I carry out in a calm, caring way that my daughters feel they can rely on and that is fun for them. Some of the "dad" things we do together at our upstate house are grilling steak, raking the lawn, cleaning the pool, making pancakes on Sunday, and drinking coffee from my cup. Setting a mood of comfort and trust—that's what my dad did for me, and that's what I aspire to do for my girls.

My father installed wood floors in every house our family lived in. He thought a highly glossed, polyurethane-covered wood floor looked plastic and cheap, and that really bothered him. He believed in celebrating the grain of wood, of old growth and new growth, and liked a floor that expressed the "board-ness" of each piece. I definitely inherited this aesthetic from him; so when it came to the floor, I had to redo it. The existing floor in the old portion of the house, which dated from 1800, had an overly glossy lamination, which was wrong on so many levels. Coincidentally, I discovered a reclaimed heart pine flooring that was being made at the time for the new Whitney Museum in New York City, and was able to join on with the massive order. I sanded and did the finishing myself—with oil, of course.

For my wife and me, Friday afternoon means gathering our daughters and dog, packing the car with our bags and groceries, and heading to the country. Leaving the city is a great feeling, but it doesn't really feel like we've escaped from New York until we've battled traffic and come around a corner out of New Paltz and see Mohonk Mountain. Then we crack the windows, the girls know we're almost home, the dog perks up, and everybody's happy.

When we pull up the long driveway, we take a walk if it's nice outside. We love to reconnect to the sights and smells of the season: skating and fires in winter; grilling outside and swimming in summer. It may be my imagination, but I'm fairly sure the sound of crickets and frogs help the girls sleep much better in the country.

CHAPTER 6

The Meaning of Making Things

The projects in this book are united by a respect for time and for the value of longevity through the use of enduring materials, whether they're used in architecture or clothing. You want to make something that lasts. With a restaurant, a good first impression is important, but a restaurant is not fleeting space. People have to connect to it in order to come back. The same thing applies to clothing: a favorite shirt ages well, fits right; it feels good, so you want to wear it again and again.

My connection with design began early. My father, Toivo, who was born in Estonia, worked as an aerospace engineer. He designed and built our wood home on Lake Orion in Michigan. If we needed a desk or a bed or a dining room table, he would build it in the woodshop that was part of our house. My mother, Tiia, a schoolteacher, also from Estonia, had a sewing room and made clothes for herself.

I didn't appreciate my father's work until I was an adult. He was so much an engineer that his furniture was so functional that it wasn't that aesthetic. I wanted to make things that connected to emotions. Regardless, I learned from him that if you need something, then you should make it yourself. And if something seems to be missing from your life, you do the same. That thing could be a piece of furniture, or a place to hang out. But the point is, if you need it or want it, then figure out a way to engineer it.

To that end, my father built a sawdust collector in order to keep his shop clean. I liked to dig in the sawdust and I still remember the smell. He is frugal—he used simple pine to build things, because he favored function and simplicity. In fact, the smell of pine still reminds me of that house and my father.

The best things you do are with your hands. I still work with the crew on restaurant projects because I feel a connection to people who do things, who solve problems, who work on-site—people whose initial instinct is to build a bookshelf if they need one, not to go online and order one. I love the first day of demolition. I enjoy being part of the build process because it's a logical extension of the design process. I don't have an office. That surprises a lot people. Whatever I design or build or design in private eventually has to connect with the public.

And what runs a restaurant, men's store, or barbershop are people. There are people you never see: they open the restaurant, sweep the floors, wash the dishes, and sew the clothes. They're a crucial part of the ecosystem of a business, which ebbs and flows. Nothing can exist without people and the roles they play. You may never see the man who power-washes Freemans Alley every morning or the line cooks who roast the chickens, but everything we do is dependent on this ecosystem, and I'm just a part of that.

In the end, it remains thrilling to design and build spaces that are used, clothes that are worn, bars where people drink, a house where my daughters are growing up. You want these places to have a sensibility, an aesthetic, a sense of craft. But, ultimately, for a place to succeed, to resonate, to embed itself in our psyches, where it is capable of stirring memory, it has to connect with people when they're close at hand.

Everything begins with a sketch, which then evolves into a more specific measured drawing. But no matter how much time you spend on the conceptual side of things, everything changes when you make an actual prototype. It's not possible to anticipate all the variables, no matter how much experience you have. I love to draw when I'm working on a piece of furniture or a room, but am now trying to build prototypes earlier in the process, because I've see how easy it is to slip into a world of drawing that never enters reality and because building earlier on lets me see what I've imagined more quickly.

COCKTAILS

FREEMANS COCKTAIL

Developed by one of our original bartenders, Toby Maloney, this is our signature cocktail. It's just strong enough, very well balanced, and not at all sweet.

2¼ ounces rye
¼ ounce simple syrup
½ ounce pomegranate molasses
   (heaping bar spoon)
¾ ounce lemon juice
2 dashes house orange bitters
Orange twist, for garnish

Shake all ingredients together, then serve in a martini glass, with a flamed orange twist.

AMERICAN TRILOGY

A complex cocktail that makes a good option for those looking for an alternative to an old-fashioned. If you have two, you'll feel it.

1 ounce rye
1 ounce applejack
1 brown sugar cube
Orange bitters (mix of Fee Brothers and Regans')
Cracked ice
Orange and lemon twists, for garnish

Combine sugar, bitters, and a splash of rye in an old-fashioned glass. Muddle sugar cube. Add remaining liquor, cracked ice, and stir. Garnish with lemon and orange twists.

FRENCH 75 (the Freemans Version)

The French 75 is one of the most refreshing drinks—and a very popular one at the restaurant. It's always on the menu.

1 ounce gin
½ ounce lemon syrup
½ ounce simple syrup
Champagne float
Lemon twist, for garnish

Shake, then strain into collins glass over ice. Fill rest of glass with champagne. Garnish with a lemon twist.

OLD PALOMINO

Developed by our former beverage director and head bartender, Yana Volfson, this is a compelling cocktail, especially for those who are partial to the smoky nature of mescal.

1½ ounces white tequila
½ ounce mescal
¾ ounce lime juice
1 ounce ginger syrup
Lime wedge, for garnish

Shake, then strain into highball glass over ice. Garnish with lime wedge.

FREEMANS BLOODY MARY

This nicely spiced version of the classic weekend drink was developed by our former bartender Jean Adamson.

2 ounces vodka
Bloody Mary mix (recipe opposite)
Caper berry, for garnish

Build in glass on the rocks. Roll drink into mixing tin. Roll back into glass. Serve in tall highball glass and garnish with caper berry.

SUMMER MANHATTAN

This is a lighter version of a classic manhattan developed by William Tigertt, and it's perfect for those who like their rye all year round. The vermouth and orange bitters make a nice counterpoint to the rye.

1½ ounces rye
1 ounce sweet vermouth
½ ounce dry vermouth
2 dashes orange bitters
Ice
Lemon twist, for garnish

Stir. Let drink sit on ice for 1 minute. Strain into chilled cocktail glass and garnish with a twist of lemon.

FREEMANS BLOODY MARY MIX

12 16-ounce cans tomato juice
4 10-ounce bottles Worcestershire sauce
50 dashes balsamic vinegar
30 dashes Tabasco
36 ounces (³/₄ of 48-ounce jar) caper-berry brine
¼ cup celery salt
1,000 turns of pepper mill
12 soup spoons of Dijon mustard
½ cup fresh horseradish

Mix all ingredients in a large bucket. Stir and refrigerate overnight.

THE RUSTY KNOT

At the Rusty Knot, many of the cocktails are frozen and made in a blender—they're easygoing, and that's the spirit of the place. It's all about watching the sunset and listening to Christopher Cross.

2 ounces Flor de Caña 4 Year Gold
2 ounces house-made sour mix (see opposite)
1 ounce simple syrup
5 dashes Angostura bitters
8 to 10 mint leaves

Blend with ice, serve in a highball glass.

SPICED COLADA

On our menu since we opened, this drink is a slightly elevated take on the piña colada.

2 ounces Cruzan 9 Spiced Rum
2 ounces house-made sour mix (see opposite)
3 ounces colada mix (see opposite)
Angostura bitters, for garnish

Blend with ice and shake Angostura bitters over top.

ZOMBIE

The Zombie is probably the fruitiest drink we serve, yet it is not too sweet, thanks to the bitters in the mix. But the rum doesn't hurt either.

2 ounces Brugal white rum
2 ounces house-made sour mix (see opposite)
2 ounces Zombie mix (see opposite)

Shake well and serve in a highball glass.

HOUSE-MADE SOUR MIX

Produces 1 liter, for roughly 15 drinks

1 cup fresh-squeezed lime juice
1 cup fresh-squeezed lemon juice
2 cups simple syrup
1 ounce Tito's vodka
1 ounce orange juice

Combine ingredients in a bowl and stir well.

COLADA MIX

Produces 1 liter, for roughly 10 Spiced Coladas.

22 ounces Coco López cream of coconut
6 ounces pineapple juice
6 ounces simple syrup
1 ounce fresh lime juice
1 ounce Tito's vodka
½ ounce Angostura bitters

Combine ingredients in a bowl and stir well and refrigerate for 30 minutes.

ZOMBIE MIX

Produces 1 liter, for roughly 15 drinks

15 ounces passion fruit puree
7½ ounces papaya puree
4 ounces apricot liquor
7 ounces simple syrup
1 ounce Tito's vodka
7½ ounces Peychaud's bitters
⅓ ounce Angostura bitters

Combine ingredients in a bowl and stir well and refrigerate for 30 minutes.

THIRD EYE

This experimental cocktail features Kronan Swedish Punsch. Reminiscent of good aged rum, it's well balanced and not at all sweet.

1½ ounces Kronan Swedish Punsch
¾ ounce Atxa pacharán
½ ounce Pineau des Charentes
½ ounce lemon juice
Star anise, for garnish

Combine in a shaker, shake, strain into a coupe glass, and garnish with star anise.

THE BLACK LODGE

Creating Scotch-based cocktails are a chance to play on a familiar taste and cut its intensity. Cynar, a bittersweet, herb-infused Italian liqueur, is a surprising addition here, making the Black Lodge a compelling, worthwhile gamble.

¾ ounce Bank Note (or preferred blended Scotch)
¼ ounce Ledaig Aged 10 Years Single Malt Whisky
   (or preferred Islay single malt)
1 ounce Amaro Montenegro
1 ounce Cynar
Orange twist, for garnish

Stir ingredients in a mixing glass, strain over rocks in a rocks glass, and serve with a flamed orange twist.

HAWK WIND

The interaction between the heat and richness of the bourbon and the aromatic complexity of the Cardamaro and Elisir Novasalus gives this drink interest.

1½ ounces bourbon
¾ ounce Cardamaro
½ ounce ginger syrup
Elisir Novasalus (or Fernet-Branca),
   to rinse coupe glass
Orange twist, for garnish

Stir ingredients in a mixing glass, strain into rinsed coupe, serve with an orange twist.

THE EQUAL DEAD

This drink is a smoky pleasure that brings some heat, thanks to Ancho Reyes, a chili liqueur. The Ancho Reyes is the star here, but it should be used with discretion.

1½ ounces mescal
½ ounce Ancho Reyes
½ ounce cinnamon simple syrup
2 drops Bittermens Xocolatl Mole Bitters
Cinnamon stick, for garnish

Stir ingredients in a mixing glass, strain over rocks in a rocks glass, garnish with a cinnamon stick.

RECIPES

ARTICHOKE DIP

When we started Freemans, I wanted to include this artichoke dip on the menu. Our first cook, Chloe Osborne, initially refused to make it; she wanted the dip to be fancier. But I insisted—and it's always been our most popular dish.

TIME: 45 minutes
SERVES: 6–8

¾ cup mayonnaise (Hellmann's is best)
1 pinch of cayenne pepper
1 clove garlic
2 cans (14 ounces) artichoke hearts in water,
  drained and finely chopped
½ cup grated Parmesan cheese
1 baguette, sliced diagonally,
½-inch thick

1. Preheat oven to 425°F.
2. In a food processor, place mayonnaise, cayenne, and garlic. Process until smooth.
3. Add half the artichokes and half the cheese, pulse to combine. Place in a bowl, and fold in the remaining artichoke and cheese.
4. Transfer to a 1-quart baking dish. Bake until golden and bubbly, about 30 minutes.
5. Lay out bread slices on a cookie sheet and toast until golden, about 5 minutes.
6. Serve everything hot.

DEVILS ON HORSEBACK

This is another Freemans favorite; it's been on the menu since we opened.

TIME: 30 minutes
SERVES: Quantities needed for this recipe depends on how many people you want to serve. I recommend at least 2 pieces per person, but certain people eat many, many more than two.

Pitted prunes
Block of buttermilk blue cheese
Bacon, preferably thick cut, into ¼-inch-thick slices
Toothpicks

1. Preheat oven to 425°F.
2. Cut blue cheese into ½-inch cubes. It helps to heat the knife by running it under hot water and drying it off. Any crumbles can be smashed together to use.
3. Stuff blue cheese into the prune hole (where the pit used to be).
4. Wrap bacon around the prune and secure with toothpick. If using thick bacon, overlap the strip only enough so it can be secured. If using a thinner cut of bacon, double wrap the prunes.
5. Bake until bacon is fully cooked, about 15 minutes.

HUNTER'S STEW

This seemed like something that fit well with the restaurant, and like what would be eaten before spending all day outside. It appears on the menu only in the winter.

TIME: 4 hours, largely unattended
SERVES: 6–8

5 cloves garlic
2 large celery roots
2 large Spanish onions
4 Yukon Gold potatoes
1½ pounds venison stew meat*
1½ pounds elk stew meat
1½ pounds wild boar stew meat
Salt and pepper, to taste
Chicken or pork stock as needed, about 3 quarts
2 sprigs fresh rosemary
5 sprigs fresh thyme
5 sprigs fresh sage
½ bottle full-bodied red wine

1. Slice garlic and coarsely dice the celery roots and onions. Place potatoes in water to help remove some of the starch. (Any amount of soaking helps keep the potatoes from becoming gummy.)
2. In a large pot, sear the meat in batches, making sure not to overcrowd the meat. At this stage, the goal is to get good Maillard reaction color on the meat; it is not necessary to cook it completely. Season meat with salt and pepper while it is searing.
3. Reserve the meat on a plate and cover it. In the same pot used for the meat, place the garlic, celery root, and onion and allow to cook until soft and the onion is translucent. Season with salt.
4. Add the wine to the pot and allow it to reduce by half.
5. Add the meat back into the pot, cover with stock. Bring to a gentle boil, then reduce to simmer.
6. Cook for about 1 hour, skimming off any fat or foam that rises to the top.
7. Add the potatoes and the herbs to the pot. Continue to cook until potatoes are tender and meat falls apart when touched. Taste, and adjust seasoning as needed.
8. Serve in warmed bowls, topped with herbed yogurt (recipe below); and mashed potatoes or crusty bread on the side.

*If game meat is unavailable, lamb or beef are suitable substitutes, though not nearly as interesting.

HERBED YOGURT FOR HUNTER'S STEW

TIME: 45 minutes
MAKES: 2½ cups

1 sprig fresh rosemary
1 sprig fresh oregano
1 clove garlic
1 shallot
1 pinch of paprika
½ cup extra-virgin olive oil
2 cups thick Greek yogurt
Salt and pepper, to taste

1. Pick the leaves off the herb stems and chop. Slice the garlic and shallot.
2. In a saucepan, gently heat the olive oil, and fry the herbs, garlic, shallot, and paprika until fragrant, about 3 minutes.
3. Allow mixture to cool completely.
4. Fold mixture into yogurt, and season with salt and pepper. Yogurt is best after several hours, so make ahead of time if possible.

MASHED POTATOES

Mashed potatoes are like scrambled eggs—everybody can make them, but there's a wide range of how successful they are. It's reassuring to see on a menu.

TIME: 1 hour + at least 1 hour for soaking
SERVES: 6–8

2 pounds Idaho potatoes
2 pounds Yukon Gold potatoes
3 cups heavy cream
1 stick butter
3 cloves garlic, peeled and minced
Salt and pepper, to taste

1. Peel the Idaho potatoes and cut into thirds. Leave the skin on the Yukons but also cut them into thirds. Place both batches of potatoes in water and allow them to sit for at least one hour (and up to 8 hours), in order to remove the starch. Any amount of soaking helps keep the potatoes from becoming gummy.
2. Drain the potatoes and place them in a large pot. Cover with cold water. Bring to a boil over medium-high heat but turn down to medium as the water begins to bubble. Cook until the potatoes are tender, about 20 minutes.
3. Meanwhile, put the cream, butter, and garlic into a smaller pot. Heat over low heat. Watch the pot, if it starts to boil, it will bubble over and make a mess.
4. Drain the potatoes into a colander, and put the potatoes back in the pot. Mash the potatoes with a potato masher. Add the cream-butter mixture a little at a time to help with the mashing process, until the potatoes are mostly smooth and creamy. Remember to not overwork the potatoes and that they will thicken naturally as they sit. Season heavily, to taste.

FRIED CHICKPEAS

This is an improved, more decadent version of a dish
I make at my house upstate. I bake the chickpeas.
Here, the chickpeas are soaked overnight, then fried—
they're terrific.

TIME: 30 minutes + overnight marinade
SERVES: 4

2 cups dried chickpeas
1 lemon
1 medium yellow onion
1 head garlic
1 cup extra-virgin olive oil
½ cup salt, plus 1 teaspoon
2 tablespoons cumin seed
2 tablespoons coriander seed
2 tablespoons smoked paprika
1 teaspoon white sugar
2 quarts fryer oil

1. Place chickpeas, lemon, onion, and garlic in a large pot
   of water (about 8 cups) and bring to a simmer until the
   chickpeas are cooked through, roughly 30 minutes.
2. Pour the chickpea mixture into a glass container and
   add ½ cup salt and olive oil. Let cool in liquid overnight
   in the refrigerator.
3. Toast cumin and coriander seed in a low temperature
   oven. Then, in a spice grinder, blend with paprika,
   sugar, and teaspoon of salt and set aside.
4. Strain cooked chickpeas so they are dry.
5. Preheat fryer oil in a large pot to 350°F.
6. Fry chickpeas one cup at a time until they are
   golden brown.
7. Take the chickpeas out of the fryer and mix in
   the spice mixture.

FINGERLING POTATOES
WITH CHARRED JALAPEÑO AIOLI

This is another dish that's an improved version of
something I make myself. The more smashed the better.

TIME: 1 hour
SERVES: 4

1 pound Russian banana fingerling potatoes
2 egg yolks
1 cup chopped cilantro
2 peeled and seeded charred jalapeños
1 tablespoon Dijon mustard
1 pint grape-seed oil
Zest of 1 lime, plus 2 tablespoons
 fresh-squeezed juice
Salt, to taste
1 cup Maldon salt
Zest of 1 lemon
1 quart fryer oil

1. Boil potatoes in salted water until tender. Let them cool.
2. Place yolks, cilantro, jalapeños, and mustard in a food
   processor and blend on high. Slowly incorporate the
   grape-seed oil until emulsified.
3. Zest lemon and lime with a microplane and mix with
   Maldon salt. Set aside.
4. Add lime juice and salt, to taste.
5. Preheat fryer oil in a large pot to 350°F.
6. Smash the cooked potatoes with the palm of your
   hand or the side of a chef knife and break up into
   smaller pieces.
7. Fry a handful of potatoes at a time until crispy.
8. Toss the potatoes directly with the citrus salt and serve
   with the charred jalapeño aioli.

KALE CAESAR SALAD WITH CHIA SEED CRISP

I'm obsessed with kale and I don't care who knows it. I honestly like the way it tastes. We tried to grill the kale and that ended up, literally, in flames. This is less hazardous and tastes better.

TIME: 45 minutes
SERVES: 2

1 anchovy filet
2 cloves garlic
¼ cup grated Parmesan, plus more for garnish
2 tablespoons fresh-squeezed lemon juice
1 egg yolk
1 teaspoon Dijon mustard
1 pint grape-seed oil
⅔ teaspoon salt, plus more to taste
Pepper, to taste
1 teaspoon chia seeds
1½ cups flour
⅓ cup water
½ tablespoon extra-virgin olive oil
2 grams fish sauce
4 cups finely cut Tuscan kale

1. Preheat the oven to 325°F.
2. Place anchovy, garlic, Parmesan, lemon juice, yolk, and mustard in a food processor and turn on high. Slowly emulsify grape-seed oil until combined and add salt and cracked black pepper, to taste.
3. Place chia seeds, flour, water, olive oil, ⅔ teaspoon of salt, and fish sauce in a bowl and whisk together. Let set for 15 minutes.
4. On a sheet tray covered with parchment paper, spread out the mixture in an even thin layer. Bake until crisp and golden brown, 15 to 20 minutes.
5. Dress the cut kale with the Caesar dressing in a bowl. Crumble the chia seed crisp over the top and then grate fresh Parmesan to finish.

BREAKFAST PIZZA WITH COPA AND SALSA VERDE

This is one of my favorite dishes. I liked the idea of a dish for stoners, but more elevated. Who doesn't love pizza, eggs, and bacon? This is the ultimate hangover dish.

TIME: 30 minutes + overnight marinade
SERVES: 2

¼ cup chopped mint
¼ cup chopped flat-leaf parsley
¼ cup chopped cilantro
2 anchovy filets, chopped
Zest of 1 lemon
2 cloves garlic, chopped
2 cups extra-virgin olive oil
2 tablespoons chopped capers
12-inch pizza dough
¼ grated fontina cheese
2 eggs
4 slices of good-quality cured copa

1. In a bowl, mix mint, parsley, cilantro, anchovies, lemon zest, garlic, olive oil, and capers and let sit in the refrigerator overnight. Remove the next day, and let sit for an hour before making the pie.
2. Preheat a pizza stone in the oven at 550°F.
3. Stretch the pizza dough to 12 inches. Place cheese and copa on the top and put the pie in the oven.
4. After a couple of minutes, open the oven and crack the 2 eggs on top of the pizza. Bake until the whites are cooked; the yolks should not be totally cooked.
5. Remove and place on a plate. Drizzle the salsa verde over the top.

CHICKEN WITH PAPRIKA LIME VINAIGRETTE

ISA has a wood oven, which really transforms this specific dish, but it's a great recipe for any home chef nonetheless. It reminds me of my dad, who used to smoke chickens in our backyard.

TIME: 1 hour + overnight marinade
SERVES: 2–4

2 half chickens
2 cups salt for the brine
1 cup sugar
3 sprigs fresh thyme
1 branch fresh rosemary
1 head garlic
6 chiles de arbol
1 shallot, diced
1 tablespoon sweet paprika
2 tablespoon fresh-squeezed lime juice
Salt and pepper, to taste
5 tablespoon extra-virgin olive oil
Grapeseed oil
3 tablespoon chopped cilantro

1. Boil 1 gallon of water with the salt, sugar, thyme, rosemary, garlic, and chiles, then let cool in the refrigerator. Once it's cool, place chicken inside the brine and let stand for 24 hours in the refrigerator.
2. Place shallot, paprika, lime juice, and a pinch of salt in a small bowl for 30 minutes, then add the olive oil.
3. Heat oven to 425°F and preheat a cast-iron pan. Take chicken out of the brine and pat dry. Season with salt and pepper, to taste. Add a little bit of grape-seed oil to the hot pan and then place chicken skin side down. Cook in the oven 8 to 10 minutes, until golden brown, then flip it and cook until it reaches an internal temperature of 165 degrees, about another 8 minutes.
4. Take out of the oven and let rest for 10 minutes.
5. Cut the half chicken into two to four pieces and toss in a bowl with the lime-paprika vinaigrette and chopped cilantro.

Working on this book has made me remember how, when it came to creating an object, or piece of furniture, or a space, I used to think and plan a lot, but then I wouldn't actually make anything. I spent my time worrying, deliberating, and making master plans. One day, out of frustration, I decided I had to change that. I started thinking about how great I felt when I let my primal instincts take over, when I would ride a bike through the woods, snowboard out of bounds, and skateboard down an unfamiliar street.

That's when I decided to stop thinking so much and start doing more. I had never worked in a restaurant or a clothing company; I had never run a barbershop or a bar or any other business. I didn't know how to be a father or a husband. But then I started to do these things. I made mistakes of course, but that's all part of the process. I realized that I couldn't be afraid to fail and fail often.

The fear of failure and pain used to paralyze me into inactivity, left me stranded in the safety of thinking, of my head. Today, I still like to dream and plan, but I try to keep it to a minimum and get into the realm where instinct, thought, and action merge. I watch my daughters live fearlessly every day—they are already prolific artists, dancers, actors, storytellers, bosses, singers, and detectives. Sadly, that instinct to do and explore often feels diminished as we grow older, as we grow more educated, as we grow more worldly. But listening to and acting on instinct is still deeply wired within all of us: it's just a matter of remembering how to be free.

ACKNOWLEDGMENTS

This book—and all the spaces featured in it—were created through great collaboration. I'd like to thank the many people who brought their talent, commitment, and efforts to make everything a reality.

Many thanks to:

The craftsmen, woodworkers, contractors, and plumbers who made these immense projects real with their own hands.

Our publisher, Harper Design, particularly executive editor Elizabeth Sullivan, for her tireless support of this project from beginning to end. She took a chance on our unique working approach, and we're very grateful.

Mark Noë and his visionary team at Noë & Associates, who designed the book.

David Prince and his team who took enough photographs to fill many books and wonderfully captured the spirit of the spaces. To Tuukka Koski, Gosuke Sugiyama, and

Leslie Williamson for contributing their photographs. And to Allison Connell, for her marbled paper.

My friends for advice and support, particularly my business partner William Tigertt; Serge Becker, who gave me my start in New York; my longtime compadre Carlos Quiarte; and my coauthor and friend David Coggins.

My father, Toivo, who nurtured the importance of following one's passion, and to my mother, Tiia, who instilled in me the love of the world of art and culture.

My lovely wife, Courtney, who has been with me since we lived in a tiny apartment on Second Avenue. She brings grace and a sense of humor to everything we do together. To our lovely young daughters, Tessa and Isla, who are my sweetest and fiercest critics.

Finally, on the following pages are the names of the many people who have helped bring all these places to life every day since we opened our doors. My deep thanks goes to them all.

Kabore Abdoulaye-Yago / Zaakirah Abdullah / Alvaro Acevedo / Diallo Adama /
Jean Adamson / Arielle Adamy / Nurul Kabir Adnan / Andrew Adolph / Ignacio Aguilar /
Jessica Allen / Jorge Alvarez-Tostado / Alex Amay / Shahin Amirizadeh / Zan Amparan /
Zina Anaplioti / Jeremy Anderegg / Samuel Anderson / Casiano Andrade-Abat /
Blake Andrews / Ugochukwu Anyanwu / Lisa Anziano / Richard Armstrong / John Arnos /
Ruben Aronov / Christina Arroyo / Marc Arthur / Craig Atlas / Leobardo Avila /
Manuel Ayala / Issouf Ba / Joaquin Baca / Michael Bachelet / Aka Badara / Ismael Bajaha /
Christopher Baker / Elizabeth Baker / Touwende Balma / Robert Banat / Marshall Bang /
Madeline Barasch / Kristine Barilli / Adrian Barrera / Jessica Barrett / Ismael Barri /
Angela Barrow / Ted Barrow / Zachary Barrow / Abdoul Raoul Barry / Dmitri Bartlett /
Byron Bates / Oba Iman Battle / Alberto Bautista / Jose Bautista / Robert Baxley /
Michael Beatty / Kevin Beckett / Courtney Bednarowski / Randolph Belandria /
Matthew Belanger / Lesley Benard / Katie Bender / Spencer Bergen / Arielle Berman /
Kathryn Berringer / Sherry Berrios / Gabriel Berrios-Gomez / Ama Birch / Daniel Birnbaum /
Larissa Blackford / Katherine Blake / Brookes Blalock / Serena Blanchard / Samuel Bland /
Juan Bocca / Elanor Bock / Jason Bois / Sixto Bonilla / Emilio Bonilla Teco /
Julien Bonnouvrier / Jake Boyle / Martin Bradley / Kathryn Bradshaw / Eric Brammer /
Jesse Breneman / Katrina Brenner / Peter Brensinger / Alicia Breslin / Evan Briggs /
Bendict Brink / Maxwell Britten / Erika Broad / Sam Brody -Felber / Cara Brooke /
Michelle Brotherton / Mathieu Brown / Wynyard Brown / Wojciech Brzozowski /
Tom Budny / Cammisa Buerhaus / Cassandra Bugge / Emily Burke / Fowzy Butt /
Gerardo Cabrera / Michelle Cagianese / Luis Cajilema / Robert Calabrese /
Gregorio Milan Calderon / Juan Calderon Perez / Fernando Calderon Ramirez /
Bambo Camara / Mody Camara / Jonathan L. Cammisa / David Campos / Baldemar Candia /
Euclides Candia / Fortino Candia / Gilberto Candia / Ivan Candia / Colin Cannon /
Mariano Cano / Rodrigo Cano / Noel Cantu / Paulino Cantu Guzman / Zachary Capito /
Cruz Capulin / Gabriel Capulin-Ramos / Mindy Cardozo / John Carmenatty /
Antonio Carmona / Sarah Carosi / Jesus Carpio / Edgar Carrasco Cantu / Joseph Casale /
Josue Casique Rivera / Abreu Olivo Casmiro De Jesus / Carina Cass / Francisco Castellano /
Rachel Castillo / Angelica Cautu / Josh Cave / Yankuba Ceesay / Luis Cepeda /
Julia Cerbone / Brian Chan / Stephanie Chance / Karen Chandler / Wolf Chartrand /
Luis Chauca / Israel Chavela / Angelica Chavez / Hugo Chavez / Juan Chavez /

Raphael Chavez / Samuel Chavez / Sibanauus Cheeseman / Peter Chen / Zhan Chen / Craig Chosney / Sayed Choudhury / Meredith Ciochetto / Ndiouga Cisse / Michael Citarella / Anthony Citino / Jacob Clark / Camille Clavery / Scottie Collard / Matthew Collins / Caroline Contillo / Lucas Corcino Baez / Arturo Cordova / Miguel Cortes / Harper Cowan / Stephen Coyle / Doroteo Coyote Catl / Gregoria Coyotl / Bogdan Marian Coza / John Croner / Angel Cruz / Marvin Cruz / Roberto Cruz / Wilmer Cruz / Miguel Cubillos / Martin Cuevas / Ryan Cullen / Lisa Foss Curtis / Phoebe Cutter / Sarjo Damblly / Summer Damon / Gingtean Daoheung / Erika DaSilva / Charles David / Rhys Davies-Gaetano / Austin Davila / Lindsay Dawson / Pantaleon De Aquino / Leyvin De La Cruz / Dante DeBose / Arryan Decatur / Tai Decatur / Kevin DeLoach / Michael Dempsey / Georgia Dennison / Ramdai Deo / Kyle Depew / Greg Desaro / Adama Diallo / Zachary Diamond / Mahamadou Diawara / Sotirios Dimakis / Daniel Dimin / Samantha DiMora / Theresa Dinh / Ahmadou Diop / Max Doherty / Nouhou Dolley / Sergio Dolores / Gina Dos Santos / Steve Doucakis / Mamadou Drammeh / James Drescher / Natalie Drew / Kelsi Dulin / Hayden Dunham / Haley Dunn / Jonathan Dupuy / Celeste Dupuy-Spencer / Kai Earthsong / Eliott Edge / Kenneth Edwards / Andrew Egelhoff / Casey El Koury / John Embry / Alejo Emilio / Laurent Empereur / Morgan Enfield / Sam Eric / Jesus Escareno / Lars Espeland / Anderson Espinal Pena / Javier Espinosa / Stefanie Etow / Victor Everitt / Sean Fahey / Khadim Fall / Emily Farris / Diego Fernandez / Scott Fischer / Sophia Fitch / Anna Fitzgerald / Ryan Fitzgerald / Angel Flores / Kerri Florian / Sesay Foday / Mory Fofana / Chantel Footman / Thalia Forbes / Catherine Fordham / Marina Forte / Arthur Fox / Vincent Fraissange / Samuel Frances / Devonn Francis / Jamie Fredricks / Jonathan Freeland / Daniel Freienmuth / Natalie Freihon / Elizabeth French / Douglas Friedman / Jameel Frith / Elizabeth Fritts / Manuel Fuentes / Leigh Gallagher / Kelly Gallmann / Jonathan Galvan Velasco / Adama Gamene / Matthew Ganser / Daniel Garcia / Derek Garcia / Javier Garcia / Wilver Garcia / Zacarias Garcia Diaz / Seth Garrison / Janine Gay / Chika George-Ugboaja / Nate Gerloff / Ivan Geronimo / Andrew Geske / Simon Gifford / Jobani Gil / Sierra Gilboe / Paul Gilces / Maria Gilhooley / Alexandria Giroux-Dorholt / Keith Gleichenhaus / Jack Glenn / Chris Gliege / Dennis Godoy / Jessica Gold / Todd Goldstein / Katherine Golob-Jones / Adrian Gomez / Natividad Gomez / Ellen Gomory / Dylan Gonzalez / Joya Gonzalez / Oscar Gonzalez /

Erick Gonzalez Antonio Pedro Gonzalez-Mendez / Emma Goode / Daniel Gower /
Apolonio Grande / Monai Grant / Nicholas Grasa / Ashley Greene / Kayleigh Griffin /
Beth Grinberg / Russell Groh / Jionet Grullon / Christopher Guaman / Cherif Mamadou Gueye /
Agustin Gutierrez / Jose Gutierrez / Diego Guzman / Edgar Guzman / Gustavo Guzman /
Oscar Guzman / Gaudencio Guzman Parra / Tsering Gyurmey / Cory Haines / Emily Hale /
Kabore Hamidou / Zachary Hamilton / Michael Hammond / Michelle Hanna /
Jeffrey Hanset / Maya Harakawa / James Hardeman / James Harley / Mario Haro /
Kanazoe Harouna / Garth Harpole / Kelly Harris / Ana Harrison / Ryan Hart /
Anisa Hasani / Caryne Hayes / Liam Haynes / Marcus Hedgpeth / Cortney Hedlund /
Myesha Henderson / Erica Henegen / Edgar Hernandez / Marcos Hernandez /
Matias Hernandez / Jose Hernandez Ortega / Pedro Hernandez Velasquez /
Diego Hernandez-Lopez / Jane Herro / Justine Hidalgo / William Hinds / Mark Hoadley /
Josh Hobson / Esme Hoffman / Anna Margaret Hollyman / Daniel Horner / Amanda Horrigan /
Brian Horta / Benjamin Hout / Leif Huckman / Evan Hungate / Rachael Hunt /
Amber Ibarreche / Zon Ibrahim / Therry Ilboudo / Heather Immoor / Keith Inglis /
Nehajul Isalm / Malcolm Jackson / Christine Jaeger / Jennifer James / Cyle Jandreau /
Kevin Jaszek / Samuel Jayne / Arnaud Jean-Baptiste / Greem Jellyfish Hai-Pa Lee /
Mikeah Ernest Jennings / Nabor Jeronimo / Santiago Johannsen / Bryan Johnson /
Dominic Jones / Joella Jones / Spencer Dempsey Jones / Jesse Jordan / Maria Jung /
Abel Kabore / Hubert Kabore / Ibrahim Kabore / Walker Kahn / Alexander Kallner /
Gemma Kamin-Korn / Maggie Kaminski / Alex Kapsidelis / Palyzeh Kashi / Jim Kearns /
Thomas Keelan / Erin Kehoe / Michael Kelly / Daniel Kent Collisson II / Amelia Kersten /
Prince Khan / Anthony Kieren / Janet Jungkwon Kim / Kevin Kinda / Oliver Kinkel /
Whitney Klann / Celeste Knopf / Jonathan Kobritz / Vural Koccaz / Aliou Koffi /
Melody Kology / Mariam Konate / Ramatou Konate / Chelsea Kopp / Kelsea Kosko /
Maria Koulioufas / Jennie Kraeger / Steven Krebuszewski / Kei Kreutler / Ivan Kuraev /
Nikolas Kyler / Jsun Laliberte / David Landgraf / Adam Lapinski / Luis Lara /
Noe Lara Gutierrez / Leticia Lara Martinez / Jason Larson / Jon Latham / Jose Laureano /
Kayla Lavelle / Gregory Lay / Sulijah Learmont / Claudia Lechuga / Jameson Lee /
Stephen Leed / Cesar Lema / William Lemon / Luis Leon / Eudoxio Leonardo /
Zachary Lewis / Ying Li / Daniel Licona Guzman / Katherine Liedtke / Natasha Liegel /
Andrew Lifschutz / Georgia Lifsher / Marcus Lightbourne / Leonelo Montesinos Lima /

Luis Linares / Helena Lind / Steven Little / Alice Liu / Josh Livingston / Arieta Lleshi /
Tiombe Lockhart Gabriel Lombardi / Antonio Lopez / Luis Lopez / Pablo Tapia Lopez /
Manuel Lora / Bronte Lord / Wilian Lovos / Jessica Lowe / Stacy Lucas / Carlos Ludizaca /
Gerardo Luna / Anastacio Luna Teco / Felipe Luna Teco / Christopher Lunney /
Shuna Lydon / Timothy J. Lynch / Daylin Machic / Lincoln Madley / Lauren Madson /
Preston Madson / Luke Makovic / Eduardo Maldonado / Matthew Mallardi / Joe Mallo /
Toby Maloney / Pedro Manzanillo / Lina Markarian / Santiago Marquez / Lynnette Marrero /
John Marshall / Katherine Marshall / Stefan Martin / Fernando Martinez /
Francisco Martinez / Jorge Luis Bautista Martinez / Margarito Bautista Martinez /
Michael Martinez / Miles Martinez / Tonatiuh Martinez / Andrew Martini / Breye Mata /
Benjamin Matthews / Michael Mauro / Julie Mauskop / Jeff McAllister / Walker McBain /
Alaska McFadden / Judah McFadden / Alexander McNeely / Jennifer McReynolds /
Ryan McReynolds / Fabiola Medina / Michelle Meged / Palemon Mejia / Roberto Mejia /
Carlos Melendez / Frank Melisi / Jose Mena / Joao Mendes / Daniel Mendez / Hector Mendez /
Geovani Mercado / Stephanie Mermis / Jakobus Michele / Mark Miguez / Jeremy Mikush /
Michael Milhausen / Gregory Mills / Jorge Miranda / Aysha Miskin / Lucy Moe /
Doug Moffitt / Terrell Molette / Jose Molina / Oscar Molina / Daniela Momo /
Ricardo Montalban / Lia Mooney / Griffin Moore / Sommer Moore / Oscar Morales /
Carlos Moreno / Diego Moreno / August Moschitto / Elan Moss-Bachrach / Artie Moyd /
Leah Mulartrick / Billy Muncy / Naomi Munro / Jack Murphy / Shannon Mustipher /
Jiovanni Nadal / Coco Nagasaka / Avinash Nagesar / Kader Nanema / Mason Nash /
Edgar Nava / Freddy Nava / Jorge Nava Gutierrez / Jose Luis Nava Gutierrez /
Raul Nava Gutierrez / Jason Necker / Steven Neff / Patricia Nelson / Antonio Neri /
Crescencio Neri Santos / Brian Nestler / Nina Netupsky / Chelsea Netzband /
Daniel Newberg / George Nguyen / Isaac Nichols / Robert Nichols / Mariano Nicolas /
Abdoul Haziz Nikiema / Alexander Nolan / Arturo Noriega / Norris / Ignacio Mattos Noya /
Jeffrey O'Keefe / Neil O'Malley / Richard Oates / Jason Obregon / Hector Ocasio /
Jennifer Odishoo / Patricia Oliva / Jhair Olivares / Kurato Ono / Jacqueline Oparah /
Laura Ornella / David Antonio Ortigoza / Kevin Ortiz / Rosendo Ortiz / Chloe Osborne /
Carlos Osorio / Pablo Osorio / Marcel Ouedraogo / Michael Ouedraogo / Raoul Ouedraogo /
Samad Ouedraogo / Wendwaoga Ouedraogo / Ashley Overholt / Peter Oviatt /
David Paarlberg / Alexander Pack / Diego Paida / Khenrab Palden / Colvito Duryea Palmore /

Luis Palomino / Romel Palomino / Kate Pane / Filipina Paras / Ben Parish /
Kristin Parker / Erin Parsch / Robert Patti / Atisha Paulson / Curtis Pawley / Allison Paz /
Patricia Peacock / Tobias Garcia Pelaez / Edgar Penaloza / Mack Peoples / Rafael Perdomo /
Diego Perez / Freddy Perez / Cameron Perkins / Margaret Perkins / Aaliyah Perpall /
Alexander Person / Brian Peterson / William Peterson / Lief Pettersson / Glenda Pezuela /
Christine Phanthe / Laura Phillips / Ginger Pierce / Elmer Pineda / Pedro Pineda /
Bruno Pinto / Wali Pittman / John Platt / Miguel Portela / Rob Portela / Lindsay Powell /
Baltazar Prado / Charlotte Prager / Jamie Proctor / William Prommasit / Martha Pundsack /
David Quon / Chris Raab / Abdur Rahman / Geetanjali Ramdeo / Abel Emilio Ramirez /
Antonio Ramirez / Cervantes Ramirez / Dixson Ramirez / Fernando Ramirez /
Gregory Ramirez / Ignacio Ramirez / Johnny Ramirez / Jose Luis Ramirez /
Miguel Ramirez / Ramon Ramirez / Elmer Ramirez Miranda / Jose Ramirez-Ruiz /
Gerber Ramos / Joruy Ramos / Juan Carlos Ramos / Richard Ratna / Alexander M. Ratner /
Desiree Razo / Saturnino Rea / Silvino Rea Sanchez / Kati Rediger / Ingrid Reichert /
Bret Reichley / Anthony Rettino / Ismael Reyes Guarneros / Randolph Riback /
Juvani Richardson / Pamela Rickard / Steffen Ringelmann / Roman Riquelme /
Rebecca Rivera Scotti / Luis Rivera-Alonso / Bailey Roberts / Lindsay Robinson /
Fernando Robles / Alberto Rodriguez / Ricardo Rodriguez / Luis Rojas / Antonio Romano /
Natalia Romano / Alberto Romero / Jacob Rose / Feleke Ross / Jacinda Ross /
Kimberly Ross / Sim Ross / Jerrod Rowan / Janine Rudzinski / Olivia Rugen / Dara Ruiz /
Joseph Ruymen / Joseph Ryan / Molly Rydzel / Carla Rzeszewski / Carlos Santiago Sabas /
Daniel Sabo / Carlos Salazar / Juan Saldivar / Roxana Salehoun / Saidou Sana /
Manuel Sanchez / Neftalli Sancheza / Omar Sanchez / Ramon Sanchez /
Christopher Sander / Ernest Sanders / Sarah Sandoval / Mohamed Sanogo /
Manuel Santiago / Alberto Santiago Lara / Lily Saporta-Tagiuri / Alexis Sarandon /
Carlos Sarmiento / Miriam Sarmiento / Bernard Sawadogo / Remi Sawadogo /
Guebre Sayiba / Daniel Schaeffer / Seth Scher / Ben Schofield / Morgan Schofield /
Sydney Schutte / Danielle Schwab / Erica Schwartzberg / Bradford Scobie /
Megan Scolaro / Cara Scozzafava / Kelly Seeman / Christopher Seestedt / Lana Seiler /
Colin Self / Cody Selman / Max Serota / Kevin Shaffer / Jesse Shapell / Daniel Shapiro /
Jessica Sharples / Inna Shats / Jordan Shavarebi / Jesse Shaw / David Sheehan /
Patrick Sheehan / Phoebe Sheldon-Dean / Aisa Shelley / Arianna Shelton / Jasper Shen /

Kevin Sheneberger / Jeff Shields / Kirsty-Lee Short / Minka Sicklinger / Ibrahima Sidibe / David Siegel / Rachel Siegfried / Javier Silva / Lucy Simic / Racine Simpore / Susannah Simpson / Noah Singerman / Saikou Sisawo / Jaime Skolfield / Garret Smith / Zulekha Smith / Clark Solack / John Somers / Fernando Soto / Kabore Soto / Gary Spencer / Skyler Spohn / Eric Sponseller / Andre Springer / Ashley Springer / Jane Srisarakorn / Bobby Stackleather / Billie Steigerwald / Dane Steinlicht / James Stephens / William Stewart / Megan Stockton / Jeremiah Stone / Raphael Stone / Jaclyn Strez / Riley Strom / Thomas Sullivan / Johnny Swet / Rios O'Leary Tagiuri / Riaz Talukder / Garry Tan / George Tang / Jamie Tao / Pavlo Taran / Phillip Taratula / Robert Tardio / Emma Tarver / Joey Tasca / Emily Tausevich / Olivia Taylor / Joseph Teeling / Amelia Telc / Eugene Terrell / Cortney Thatcher / Ryan Thatcher / Sofia Theodore-Pierce / Adele Thibodeaux / Arie Thompson / Briana Thornton / Michelle Tift / Kenta Tohara / Alicia Torello / David Torres / Elias Torres / Oscar Torres / Cesar Torres-Perez / Akim Toure Nee / Joanna Trimble / Alex Trivino / Joanna Troccoli / Gabriel True / Bully Tunkara / Ebrima Tunkara / Mohamed Turay / Russell Tyler / Sanae Ueyoshi / Saara Untracht-Oakner / Sabas Valdez / Guillermo Valencia / Margaret Valiante / Glenn Van Dyke / Oscar Vasquez Perez / Charlotte Vazquez / Armando Vega / Francisco Vega / Colleen Veit / Ian Vens / Socorro Veronica / Ben Vescovi / Gianna Vicari / Varaphong Nicky / Vichittanasan / Adam Vidal / Carlos Vidal / Frank Vigliotti / Elsa Villal / Carlos Villal Sanchez / John Villamar / Elisvan Villar / Miguel Villar Camano / Manuel Villavicencio / Yana Volfson / Jacob Wachsler / Eamon Wagner / Jill Wagner / Paul Wakefield-Chapa / Allan Walker-Hodkin / Lee Wallach / Edwin McCabe Walsh / William Walter / Ginger Warburton / Charlie Ward / Caroline Waxse / Joshua Weidenmiller / Leah Wellbaum / Alisha Wetherill / Katherine Whalen / Lindsay White / Katherine Whitehead / Jonathan Wilde / Alexandra Willey / Gretchen Williams / Graham Wilson / Joseph Wilson / Jaymee Wise / Mary Wiseman / Beau Witka / Katherine Wong / Nate Woodruff / Benjamin Wrubel / Monica Wynn / Crescencio Xelo / Kazutaka Yabe / Rel Wende Yacuba / Ferdinand Yanogo / Zachariah Yaya / Michael Yinger / Shawn Yost / Pamela Yung / Shelly Zander / Joaquin Zavala Sanchez / Abdoul Zongo / Kiswendsida Zongo / Tiko Zongo / Wendyam Zongo / Achille Zoungrana / Gregory Zuccolo

PHOTOGRAPHY AND ILLUSTRATION CREDITS

Marbled paper on book case exterior: © 2016 Allison Connell, Stone & Vein.

All sketches © 2016 Taavo Somer.

All photographs © 2016 David Prince except for: pages 24–25, 52–53, 62–63, 136:
© 2016 Tuukka Koski; 85, 86–87, 88, 90–91, 93–97: © 2016 Gosuke Sugiyama: 122–123,
126–127, 131, 132, 135, 137: © 2016 Leslie Williamson.

FREEMANS

HarperCollins books may be purchased for educational, business,
or sales promotional use. For information please e-mail
the Special Markets Department at SPsales@harpercollins.com.

First published in 2016 by Harper Design
An Imprint of HarperCollins*Publishers*

195 Broadway
New York, NY 10007
Tel: (212) 207-7000
Fax: (855) 746-6023
www.hc.com
harperdesign@harpercollins.com

Distributed throughout the world by
HarperCollins*Publishers*
195 Broadway
New York, NY 10007

ISBN 978-0-06-236789-1

Library of Congress Control Number: 2014944761

Book design by Noë & Associates and Taavo Somer

Printed in China
First Printing, 2016

TAAVO SOMER is a designer, architect, and creative cofounder of the iconic Freemans restaurant, which opened on Manhattan's Lower East Side in 2004. His projects now include bars, men's stores, a clothing line, and barbershops. He's been featured in the *New York Times*, *GQ*, *Architectural Digest*, *Vogue*, the *Wall Street Journal*, *Casa Brutus*, and *Time*. He lives in Manhattan and upstate New York with his wife and two daughters.

DAVID COGGINS, coauthor, has written extensively about men's style, art, travel, and design for numerous publications including *Esquire*, the *Wall Street Journal*, *Art in America*, and *Interview*. He is the author of the book *Men and Style* and a contributing editor at *Condé Nast Traveler*. He lives in New York.